MW01277767

Africa, Buddha

haibun

MATTHEW CARETTI

Africa, Buddha

ISBN 978-1-947271-89-0

Red Moon Press
PO Box 2461
Winchester VA
22604-1661 USA
www.redmoonpress.com

Cover: Beata Somogyi, *Tathagata Africa*
11.7" x 16.5", acrylic on paper, 2021.
In the artist's collection.
Used with permission.

first printing

For the children and caregivers
of the Amitofo Care Centers,
from whom I learned a true practice
of loving-kindness and of *ubuntu*.

I would rather seek without ever finding
Than be tucked and warm and tied to nearness,
For in the country of happiness while on this earth,
I can never be an owner, only a guest.

From "Off the Coast of Africa"
by Hermann Hesse,
trans. Sherab Chödzin Kohn

Africa, Buddha

Here to There

Following as Effect from Cause

After the monastery. After a year of pilgrimage. After a month on this final retreat. Knowing now how to not know. Plan. Expect. No money. No job. But an email from Malawi. Six years since the last. Dated weeks ago. An old friend. Also a former monastic. On the possibility of meaningful work there. Orphans. The offer of a ticket.

> ursa poised
> to scoop a bit of sea
> driftwood knots

Inside Out

The sudden everything of Yangon International Airport. Inside. And out.

> sunset runway
> crimson-clad monks
> coming, going

The slow memory of retreat. Retreat of memory. Continuing the practice. Outside. And in.

> yin and yang
> of the airport carpet
> walking meditation

Nothing lasts. Nothing is finished. Nothing is perfect. We descend toward Nairobi. I smile. Inside. Outside.

> beyond the wing
> the savannah sun
> lingers

Non-Stop

Long flight of reflection. A cloudbank becomes memory. Hope. Recalling how this life moves from there to here. Warrior to poet. Lover to monk. Recluse to wayfarer. Student to teacher to student . . .

> gratitude
> eating porridge
> with my fingers

Johannesburg

His home is much as I remember it, posh without pretension. Today though it is a crime scene.

> tsotsis[1]
> stole even
> his beers

He laments his brew and his bikes, but the widescreen is irrelevant. I recommend going without; he smiles but does not answer.

> old pine perch
> sacred ibis arrive
> at sunset

He suggests Dutch-Indonesian cuisine. Orders Heineken. We share tales of our journeys, hyperbole grown these past many years. A vegetarian meal brings to mind life in the temple.

---

1. *Tsotsi* is South African slang for "thug."

beads given
freely, happily
to my old friend

Right Livelihood

In every South African newspaper, the headline. The downgrade. The sacking of the finance minister. Moody's junk status. Yet another vote of no confidence. The beggar outside the supermarket can't read, though he understands all of this. First hand. From working construction to now sleeping in the park. The numbers most important to him have become the meals he receives in a week. The digits on the spare coins pulled from the pockets of passers-by. From me, a bit more.

> on each note
> the very end
> of Madiba's smile

Muti

The taxi rank teems with life. Young girls hawk bananas and avos. Old men tote shoe shining kits. Homebound mothers haul bundles full of groceries. And uniform-clad students enjoy frozen fruit juice after classes. Beyond this throng a bit of tented shadow. A scene like one from some not-too-distant refugee camp, where one finds always a UN canopy white on the periphery. Here in the coolness of the tent's shadow stands Prince, this the name he prefers to his given Mbulelo. Much easier, he says, for the Whites. "And classy, too!" Indeed, he claims his family is of royal stock. But as the third son, he has been relegated to his perch atop Bushbuck Hill. Here he is simply the town barber.

> soft buzz
> of the swarm
> jacaranda

Since leaving the monastery, I have paid little attention to grooming. My unkempt hair and beard fall in ringlets to the red earth. What was once brown now mostly grey. Silver, my father would have called it. Locals gather to watch. An old man approaches, wrinkles his face into a toothless smile. He wonders, explains Prince, if he might have some of my shorn locks. I look to the man and back to Prince for some clarification, but then understand the old man's last word — *muti*. A term of Bantu origin meaning the medicine of *sangomas*, or witch doctors. I nod my assent before he disappears into the crowds with a rich handful of my hair. Prince grins. "A white man's silver hair, when prepared properly, brings wealth."

> tip basket
> beneath the coins
> a prayer

Township

I am somehow of this place. And yet a complete stranger. I know it still from years as a Peace Corps Volunteer. In bits and pieces, as it knows me. I left it reluctantly, yet could not wait to go. I return eagerly, yet know I will happily depart again.

> Shatale
> home of my
> divided self

These township hovels and RDP[1] boxes cage those long ago forced to the hinterlands. Leaking roofs and hollow promises continue to mock the new dispensation. But all is not lost. There are now paved roads. And a community library.

---

1. RDP is the acronym for South Africa's post-apartheid Reconstruction and Development Programme.

the scent
of new books
nowhere to go

Game drives and world cups created illusions. Then the reality of social justice's slow advance set in. Another year ends, while the process sputters and spurts. I bow to my homestay mother's grave. Turn again toward the traditional dance.

from rough soil
the harlequin blooms
of a cactus

Houses of Stone

Yet another pilgrimage. Overland to Malawi. Now paused at the Zimbabwe-South Africa border. Visas and passports and customs checks before crossing the Limpopo River. Close by, the old railway line is now a footbridge for the masses heading south. Seeking safety and work. Perhaps a new life for their children. Somehow I trade places with them. Leave any sense of knowing and security behind.

> trestlework
> long shadows
> crossing over

Stepping down from the bus into Masvingo. Then a taxi to the ruins. A fellow traveler had derided this place — "Just some piles of rocks!" But a local poet has captured it best. "Stones, the visible end of silence."

alone into
dzimba dza mabwe[1]
morning sun

Down into the valley. Past the eastern enclosures. Looking for a sacred seam in the earth. Somewhere here on the path, requiring a brief ritual. Putting down my load. Uttering a prayer to the ancestors. Then a slow, superstitious step over it.

noonday breeze
a witch's spell
hardens into bedrock

I take in my final sunset at the western enclosure. My solitary perch this past week. Alone again with the baboons and some lingering spirits of the past. Thoughts of the future. Moving beyond the monk that I was. I uncross my legs. Stand. Stride.

moonrise
the ancient wall
mapped in lichen

---

1. *Dzimba dza mabwe* is the Shona origin of "Zimbabwe," meaning "houses of stone."

Diaspora

To Harare. Before the bus, the snail's slow trail into morning light. Swollen here and there by insoluble stops. Our own journey soon punctuated by the constancy of manned checkpoints. Cadres of low-brimmed caps. Empty pockets. A greedy smile for the only white man on the coach.

> policeman's belt
> too big stretch
> of the sky

At the lodge a fellow *murungu*.[1] His long white beard something biblical. His accent, too. He tells of his long journey here. From the Promised Land. On foot. The heat and deprivations. The beatings and abuse. Yet here he is, smiling a scatter-toothed smile. And here I am with far fewer tales of such proportion. Yet both of us in search of a new tribe.

---

1. *Murungu* is the Shona word for "white person."

how the wind
scatters the leaves
babylon night

The National Gallery is a gamble, but close by. The exhibits begin with a brief tribute to Stuart Hall's seminal essay on cultural identity, noting how we are "positioned by, and position ourselves within, narratives of the past." A fine primer for my walk downtown. Three-piece suits and tribal prints. The Raj and old Rhodesia. The struggle for freedom. And with it.

mirrored glass
the ATM queue
fractures

A Sense of Distance

The old woman in the seat beside me jumps. The bus swerves wildly. Slows. Halts. A collective sigh. Both relief and dismay. Not yet to the border with Mozambique and already a blown front tire. A scramble for the bald spare.

> wattle and daub
> sharing shade
> with goats

Two hours of collective efforts to complete the change. Just as long to the border. The customs check and secondary repairs delay us still longer. The businessman, student and bridegroom join me in willing a departure. Add a bit to the driver's kitty. Anti-heroes, we conjure a swift retreat from the setting sun.

> daylight ends
> in the Zambezi
> all our hopes

Well into the night, the drivers switch. Yet the same gospel videos continue to play. Thirty minutes. Repeat. But the high notes of the hymns fall well short of heavenly. The red of a digital clock below the speaker enflames each passing moment. Better to rest my eyes outside the dusty window.

> Good Friday
> a roadside steeple
> snags the Milky Way

The border post at Mwanza has long closed for the night when we arrive. Sleeping faces press into the bus windows. Steam their own soft pillows. I find instead a two-dollar room. Stretch out into the sounds of the brothel next door.

> bed bugs
> a trail that fades
> into morning

Mistake after Mistake,
the Unmistaken Path

I arrive in Malawi. At the orphanage. Head first to the temple. Offer three bows. Three prostrations. Three sticks of incense. Then make three wishes.

To benefit the children here.

To understand why I left the monastery.

To discover a new path.

> temple gate
> the orphan boy shoots
> and scores

The Warm Heart

Weekends at a Zen Orphanage

The children bow and chant and exercise and breakfast. Then the day. The weekend. Open. Free. The way of their ancestors.

> *Chichewa*[1]
> the warmth of
> morning maize

The quiet day into a quiet night. An occasional burst of song from the nearby village. From the road to Zomba.

> night bus
> how speed
> bends sound

I wake before the rest. Stretch. Feel the Sunday world come to life.

---

1. *Chichewa* is the official language of Malawi.

vipassana[1]
birdsong enters
the side doors

Twilight lengthens. No electricity to speed it along. The deep of the dry season. Of rivers reduced to a trickle.

load sharing[2]
candle stubs prop up
each new flame

Light comes of its own accord. No switch to turn. Only to watch from the porch. To know this moment. This little chore.

darning socks
the sudden whole
of the sun

---

1. *Vipassana* is a Pali term designating insight meditation.
2. *Load sharing* denotes the process of rolling blackouts in Malawi.

The Four Elements

We gather at the far end of the dining hall. Round a long cobble of old school desks standing in for a conference table. The early morning sun playing us in light and shadow.

Earth. The local staff always arrive first, afraid of the consequences otherwise. They sit straight-backed and stoic. Silence their cell phones.

Water. The overseas volunteers, most of them from Taiwan, march in from the kitchen. Bearing a tray of delicate teacups and two pots of tea. Pu-erh and rooibos.

Fire. The nuns, one venerable the other raw, enter after all the rest have been seated. We stand. The elder smiles. The other scowls.

Wind. The outsider. The just arrived. The one who will, perhaps, stir the leaves. Sweep clouds to and from this remote place.

"Zao an!"[1] the director greets the table. Palms pressed.

"ZAO AN!" the chorus of responses, pressing palms.

Followed by a spirited "Muli bwanji!" We are after all in Malawi, I think.

Silence and a glower or two.

Wind stirs Earth. Fire boils Water. We disagree again on the use of corporal punishment. Its intention and efficacy. I wonder aloud where discipline and compassion might meet.

> morning moon
> the first phase
> of birdsong

---

1. *Zao an* is Mandarin's "Good morning!" while *Muli bwanji* is the first question in a traditional Chichewa exchange of greetings regarding one's health.

The Principal's Principles

I am called from the Upper School to the small yard in front of the Grade 1 classroom. He is in a grand fury. I approach slowly. Singing his name. Making it into a silly tune matched by the goofy smile he's seen before. We've done this now on nearly a weekly basis. He hears me coming. Turns. And launches his first stone. I duck and press forward. Stop the song.

The Child. Tears streak Alfonso's dusty face. His cries and curses ring out. Attacks on his classmates and teachers. He is new here. Clever. Both kind and cruel in turns, the latter a result of a life that's known only poverty. Abuse. Hunger. For food and family and love.

"Muli bwanji, Alfonso," the "o" trailing off apace according to Malawian elocution. Chichewa isn't, in fact, his own tribal language. But he knows well this greeting. He doesn't respond. Settles instead his shouts into a drone of low moans.

The Moment. "Shall we go for a walk?" This a new strategy to remove the danger to other students, to teachers, to the schoolhouse windows. More low moans, but no winding up for the next volley. I am by now close enough to reach out to him, but do not. I simply dangle my hand between us. Keep it there. He knows he can make me wait. And does.

The Truth. This journey began in self-doubt. A failed monk. A simple English teacher. Past agitator of academic administrators. Now hauled unwilling to the top of the school's organizational heap. A principal looking for some code. A unifying vision based on the certainty that we all suffer while searching desperately for some elusive happiness. So perhaps this little walk we take together, hand-in-hand, will do just a bit to help us along.

> cottonball clouds
> the length of each finger
> as we point

Belt and Road

We wait. She waits, unseen, while we wait.
Surely wants us to sit so as to have to stand
again when she enters. She enters. Despite
my more stubborn tendencies, I rise. Bow.
At the monastery in Korea, I learned this
game all too well. No matter. Her scowl
remains unchanged. Always so. She sits, not
near but far. Beckons the translator, a kind
young teacher from Taiwan, to join her.

> dank wind
> uneasy buzz
> of window flies

She begins with a history lesson on the Silk
Road. Segues to a lecture on the Chinese
Belt and Road initiative. Concludes with a
rather certain assertion that the children
in the orphanage school, despite a national
curriculum rooted in English, must
prioritize learning Chinese language and
culture. Buddhist doctrine, of course, too.
The young volunteer indicates that it is now

my turn to speak. I reach for my tea. Find
my breath in my beard. Smile.

>   distant baobab
>   scratching at
>   the summer sky

I have no lessons or lectures to offer. No
assertions to maintain the status quo nor to
disrupt the protocols of this place. Instead
I tell a simple story. A local myth I learned
from one of the older children. How the
sun's daughter became the mother of man.
Worked and worked for her children,
though their want was unending. Even in
death she continued her labors, until one
day a mute daughter spoke kind words,
thus releasing her from this servitude. She
became the moon, slowly returning each
month to weep at the scheming of her
children. To fill again with the hope that
one wise daughter might become many.

>   cicada song
>   the up and down lines
>   of long ago mountains

Crèche

I recall a book I've never read titled *All I Need to Know I Learned in Kindergarten*, or something like that. So in moments of great stress and indecision, I venture to the classroom hosting our youngest orphans. They are usually well into a song or dance or art project, but whatever the endeavor it conjures a swift smile. The off-key notes, the awkward steps and the intense concentration required when urging a crayon across a blank page. The teacher seems to intuit the reason for my visits, ever increasing in number as I come to grips with the immensity of my work here. She smiles kindly, not because I am the principal, but because she is genuinely a warm-hearted young Malawian, still discovering for herself the art and craft of teaching.

> inside voices
> learning the quiet
> of compassion

The teacher makes the interruptions seem as though they were planned. Begins a game. The children teach me the rules. Remind me to play fair. I hide. They seek. It is a short game. She shifts to story time, highlighting the language and culture of Malawi. We learn that we are small, the world is big. She asks me to reveal what I've brought— milk and cookies. We learn to share. And that too many cookies are not good for our tummies. She and I spread the yoga mats. Nap time. We learn that rest is important.

> when student
> becomes teacher
> chalk dust smile

The youngest of the lot forgoes the mat and instead crawls into my lap. He is four. The orphaned son of two teen orphans who met at this very place. And who in turn left him here. He is quickly asleep. And in a moment warm urine seeps from his trousers into mine. My muted gesticulations draw the attention of the teacher, who works to stifle her rich laughter. I too shake with dismay and delight.

> day moon
> the big and small
> of wash drying

Africa Cup

Market day. Some of the older children and I venture beyond the main gate. Through the macadamia estate. Down across the stream. Then up to the village beside the main road. At the trading post, the tinkerer's shop springs to life. Remnants of a radio. An old man connects a faulty wire. Tunes to some distant pitch. The children—and I—stare into the loudspeaker.

> play-by-play
> the static after
> a missed PK

Indulgence

We decide to buy our own little radio for the orphanage. We gather. Tune to the only station available within our range. Listen to the high pitched voice penetrating our abode of little buddhas. Waves carry it from some posh resort in the south of the continent. The shepherd—the children all know his name — addresses his flock. Mixes for them a batch of discontent. Stirs it with fear. Concocts some bitter elixir. Further confuses their faith with his own commandments. And an indulgence for each worldly desire.

> daily tithe
> the African prophet
> takes a third wife

More Zen Stories

We wake at 4:30am to the tolling of the temple bell. Arrive there — three prostrations completed and kneeling silently — by 5:00am. Of course, the nuns direct the liturgy, but once a week I am invited to speak to the children. To direct them in meditation. To offer a story or two.

> residue
> of a dream
> morning mist

The first account I tell is one of my favorites. That of Ryokan and the moon. Of the poor hermit's return home. The thief's empty hands. With nothing else to give, Ryokan offers his robe, then sits naked gazing out his window. No resentment or anger. Only a heart full of kindness and a wish that he could have given the man the moon.

mosquito net
creatures big and small
safe at dawn

A few weeks later I offer a tale from my earliest engagement with Buddhism. While living in Korea, I'd befriended an old mountain monk who spoke a bit of English. Every weekend he tutored me in the Dharma. I was filled with questions drawn from the books I'd been reading. So I asked about *shunyata*. Emptiness. He smiled. Went to his back room and soon returned with a crumpled copy of the *Prajnaparamita Hrdaya*, or *Heart Sutra*. Dropped it simply into my lap. One side English. The other Korean. I read both, then asked: *Do you understand this?* He smiled again. *Not yet!*

knowing
not knowing
a deep bow

Then a bit about another hermit poet. Hanshan. Cold Mountain. His descent from hidden caves to a valley temple. Begging table scraps. Laughing with the cook at the monks' piety and misplaced practices. Refusing the obeisance and offerings of high officials. Returning to the clouds. Steep trails and dangerous cliffs. Donning his tree-bark clothes. Lying down on his grass mattress. Resting peacefully his head on a stone pillow.

crescent moon
carving into water
perfect poems

Witching Hour

The teachers who live here ask me to join them. There is no talking sense, so I listen. Test my own logic and spiritual leanings. An elder hushes the village crowd. Recounts the events of this past week. The strange lights. The disappearances. The sighting of a bloodsucker . . .

> frenzied cries
> the story takes shape
> in the fire

A priest from the nearby town steps into the wavering light. Offers a blessing. Reminds the villagers that the spirit world is in eternal struggle. Light countering dark. So those practicing malevolent *juju*,[1] he says, must be chased . . .

---

1. In Malawi, *juju* denotes either traditional healing or the use of black magic.

away
into the night
hurried footfall

He leads the faithful through the night forest. Into a sudden clearing. Soon compound walls are smashed. Thatch burned. Then the quiet crackle of embers. He whispers a prayer. Eyes upturned. Towards an afterglow . . .

of hope
each gentle ring
round the moon

The Green Husk

The old nun asks me what I had missed most about lay life. Meat? Alcohol? Girls? This was also one of the most common topics of conversation for the young monks with whom I spent a good bit of my time in Korea. Some opted to avoid these conversations, especially those who continued to harbor some doubt about renunciation. Others, like me — the only foreign monk in my cohort — engaged fully. This a way to help me better understand the mind of a Korean monastic and to expand my nascent language skills.

> a letter
> tucked in the sutra
> smells of her

The Hard Shell

The devoted teacher from Shanghai proposes marriage. The entire campus of the orphanage, save the steep cliffs to the north, is surrounded by a sprawling estate of mature macadamia trees rumored to have been planted by the British royal family when this was a Crown colony. The older children, those able to scramble surreptitiously over the high walls, most often gather some of the nuts left behind after the harvest. The teacher shows me their secret path. Chooses this place to surprise me. With a gift. A smile. Her question.

> letting down
> the complexity
> of her braids

The Seed

The beautiful volunteer from Hungary joins me for a walk. I regale her with tales of my work at the schools. How during the rainy season, the children often share their nutty contraband with friends during long dormitory chats. How today a handful arrived on my desk, along with some shy lessons about how to retrieve the seed from the pericarp. A sudden deluge interrupts the narrative. Forces us from the dirt track. The volunteer and I take refuge in a cluster of macadamias. Construct an impromptu umbrella from her silk scarf. Stand close. Laugh at the very wetness of our lives.

> first kiss
> how the rainbow connects
> here and there

The Rains of Malawi

The first clouds gather on the horizon. Then the blotting of the setting sun. The wind and sudden cool. Into a slow repose as the rains begin to speak in sonorous tongues.

> on the tin roof
> a murmur
> of evening prayers

A change in cadence. From trickle to torrent. The children and I seek shelter within the shelter. Move away from the now steady drips. A bucket here. Saucer there. Relight the damp wick of the candle.

> night thunder
> the way the spider
> avoids the puddle

Time Spent at Skillful Work

The temple dog follows me up the long flight of stairs. I bow before entering. The dog curls against the threshold. The younger orphans scurry over to offer him some belly scratches. The older children continue to clear the meditation cushions left from morning chants. The masters discuss in a near corner the plan for the day's instruction. The gilded Buddha smiles on all of this with detached benevolence.

> wind stirs
> from a whirl of hands
> before war, peace

I begin to help with the cushions. Chat up the boys and girls about today's training. About the upcoming demonstration. I express my concern to some of them about foundering studies at school. Failed exams. They offer a common shrug. One of apathy born from an attitude of *What can I do*?

In fact, they are allowed little input about their lives here. Kungfu has always been and remains a top priority. For their time spent at skillful work, as "kungfu" might be translated, the donors from Asia award great merit.

cutting through
late afternoon sun
a battle cry

Buddha on a Bike

The old door creaks open. Light filters into this storage room for perhaps the first time in many years. Here are kept the nonessential donations. Sportcoats and toys and a lifetime supply of Tupperware. Light-skinned dolls stare at us from a corner shelf, dust coating their extra-long lashes. We smile uneasily at their outstretched arms. Quickly locate behind the door our treasure. Two long boxes and one short propped against the wall. Still bearing the shipping labels from Taiwan.

> alms bowl
> each curve
> of a smile

My little helpers lug the boxes past the neighboring room — the one for the so-called "essential" donations of candles and incense and baby Buddha statues — and out into the brilliant light of Malawi's early winter. Past the new temple and to an old office we commandeer and soon dub "Buddha's Bikeshop." These boxes contain the basis for our latest undertaking. Three shiny new Giant mountain bikes. We sort the frames and connect to them the handlebars, seatposts, pedals and wheels. We pump a good blast of air into the tubes, drip some lube on the chains, and the orphans are off!

> on a bike
> even a buddha
> teeters

No scraped knees or elbows. But too many close calls. The adult in the room had forgotten to ask if the children could even — had ever even — ridden a bike. So a swift retreat with all the bikes and kids to the central square. A lesson. Lots of supporting hands and gentle nudges. Mixing Chichewa, English and Mandarin,

as well as ample body language, to explain.
And again they are off. Stable pedalstrokes
and adept braking. The straight lines are
soon mastered. Together we learn slowly
how to take the turns.

a new sutra
the rolling lilt
of the sun

She makes me an offer I can refuse. So I say no before I say yes. Then change my mind, but end up changing it again. Or having it changed. The NGO's visiting director convinces and cajoles. She is after all a Zen nun quite certain of her own inherent wisdom. She plans for me a retreat to strengthen my resolve, then announces I will leave the schools at this orphanage to direct the operations at another. From the Warm Heart of Africa to the Kingdom in the Sky. As happens at a place such as this, news of this coming transfer travels quickly. Ceremonies are arranged to make the farewell official. And where in Africa there is a formal gathering, there are speeches. Many of them. Mine the last. So there in the great hall, with my final words, an unyielding reminder to the children — and a tacit scolding meant for some of our more pious overseas volunteers — *Don't worry about being a Buddhist. Just work on becoming a buddha.*

> sudden squall
> incense smoke swirls
> into nothing

Towards the Sky

A Different Word for It

After more than a year in Malawi, this long
retreat. I finish my porridge. Offer a prayer
of thanks. Raise my head. Smile.

> temple kitchen
> nourished by the Dharma
> a wayward monkey

Wash my bowl. Dry my hands. Enter the
forest. Exit into the light.

> stupa sutra
> each day
> my new voice

Descend into the valley. Pause often. Turn.
Observe. Smile again and again.

> *wild dagga*[1]
> on each flower the sun
> then a sunbird

1. *Wild dagga*, also known as Lion's Tail, is a flow-
ering shrub native to southern Africa with possible
medicinal qualities.

Farther toward the trickling brook. Along one fold of steep meadow. Onto another. The sound rising, falling with each turn of the trail.

> Zulu cowherd
> between the whistles
> the clicks

The sun warms the herd. My back. Past the docile beasts to the climb. The dam. The little jetty of my meditation.

> floating
> the duck the pond
> shimmers

Something mystical. Yet that not quite the word for it. Returning again and again. I dilate my lexicon. Seek the expression. Instead learn to express the seeking.

> evening ridge
> a sangoma speaks
> with the wind

No Place for Evil

With rounded walls, there is no place for darkness. For shadows. For the evil spirits that might lurk in corners. This the tradition of building among the many tribes of southern Africa. Homes and churches and meeting places. And as the Dharma is universal, monasteries too.

> Buddha nature
> bees hive
> in the temple eaves

Workers circle away in search of precious nectar. Toward the halleria lucida. The tree fuchsia. There in the great forest, where a shadowed path softens underfoot.

> yoga sutra
> the eucalypts bend
> toward first light

The trail opens into meadow. Descends to the Nalanda Rocks, aged through millennia into a soft roundness. A Zulu grandmother passes. Her face painted in white. Arcs and circles, just as the news travels here. Word of mouth. Already in the distant village the sound of gospel. A memorial ceremony.

> Ufafa valley
> slow glide of
> Amen

The village rondavels a palette of greens and blues and oranges. Perched high above the gorge. Swirling ridgelines descend steep into some navel of our becoming. Gentle, rounded walls. No place for evil. Yet, as in all places on this Earth, darkness does arrive. As does hope.

> *woza moya*[1]
> a grey heron becomes
> the horizon

---

1. *Woza moya* literally means "spirit wind" in Zulu, but is often used to translate the Christian "Holy Spirit."

This Windswept Place

We are nearly there. My new home. A few subsistence farms. No trees. Dust and dirt devils. Yet still there is life. Early. The sort that reminds us of our beginnings.

> morning birds
> chatter
> of the village girls

It is easy to trace origins and endings here. Open vistas. Distant horizons. An endless sky. Songs and soft voices coming and going. Later I follow the same footpath. Discover a sheltered hollow. A home.

> single track
> of the wheelbarrow
> stopping here

Settling In

Scorpio descends like a trident toward the western horizon. The Southern Cross already sunken into true south. I walk alone to the temple. Where the children sit by now in neat rows. Warm. Silent. I wonder, *What else can I give them?*

> daybreak
> lifting the burden
> of this new life

The sun rises into a cloudless sky. Cerulean. We recite morning vows. Breakfast. Receive the warm porridge as medicine for our weakening bodies. Move out into the day. Greet the new warmth.

> *seana marena*[1]
> gentle wave
> of the shepherd

1. *Seana marena*, or Basotho blankets, are the traditional colorful, wool (now often fleece) mantles worn by herders in Lesotho. They have more recently become known worldwide via the film *Black Panther*.

His mixed herd of sheep, donkeys and cows. From the Ha Chopho village on the ridge above us. Along the border fence to the endless plateau fronting the orphanage. He follows them. White gumboots on ruddy earth.

        slow trickle
        of the cold stream
        bitter aloe

The antipodal winter. At 4000 feet. Cool days. Frigid nights. Windswept. When windows slam shut. Curtains are drawn. Blankets unfurled. And the main gate bolted against all ill will.

        dark screech
        of the grass owl
        orphans sleep

Hero

I quickly come to learn how the children love animals. Surrogates for either some real or imagined affection that was lacking in their home. So they pester the lazy dogs by the gate with hugs and kisses. Keep tiny field mice in boxes under their beds. And one brave boy captures a juvenile grass owl. Trains and feeds it. Keeps it hidden in the old laundry room.

> a rustle
> in the hedge
> chasing geckos

But Wooji, "Hero" in Mandarin, is different. Special. We wonder how he came to be here. Quietly at home inside our orphanage walls. Beside our hostels and in our gardens. Some unlikely mascot. Stubborn and proud. Yet wandering again and again toward the main gate. Longing for something else.

ornery old mule
inside the evening storm
his bray

American Independence Day in Lesotho

The TV room is new. The one hundred channels of satellite connectivity strictly supervised. Screen time limited. Only the older ones allowed in. And yet the children are happy here. The NGO decided they need to know the world. Current events. News. So we shiver together in the antipodal winter. Watch a segment on the separation of immigrant families at America's southern border. They know this is my homeland. Turn to me. A sudden sorrow in their eyes. In my own.

fourth of july
orphans unravel
a stars & stripes scarf

The Binding String

The orphan's old sweater becomes a long string. Becomes the towline for a makeshift car. Of wire, bottlecaps, cardboard and saliva glue. Then abandoned becoming a plaything of the wind.

> evening sun
> wondering where
> the contrail goes

Triple Refuge

The week becomes weekend. A chance to move beyond the walls of the orphanage. Ponder the wide-open spaces. The ancient mountains.

> first church
> tilt of *Morija*[1]
> in the winter sky

Then another trip. Sunday to the capital. But before the main road, the rutted path and village farms. The toil of subsistence. The children watch. We go. And shop.

> drawn
> by mules
> an old Ford

---

1. Founded in 1833, *Morija* is site of the first French Protestant mission in Lesotho.

Some semblance of *ubuntu*.[1] I gaze around me at the other volunteers. Are we here to save or to serve? Ourselves or others? *I am because we are.* We are what?

> Maseru
> from each shanty
> a tether of smoke

Back on campus. The children smile and wave. Some press palms. Bow. I wonder how we've confused them. *Who is Buddha? What is Dharma? Where is Sangha?*

> three-legged pot
> the blackening
> of sundown mountains

---

1. A term of Bantu origin, *ubuntu* means "humanity," but is more widely used to describe the interconnected nature of all beings.

Bone of My Bones

The head of our outreach services marries.
And her preacher is a firebrand. "It is not
good for a man to be alone." He switches
to Sesotho. Loses me. Gains from the rest a
tentative "Amen."

> citing Genesis
> hollow ring
> of the cleft bell

He goes on. Eve from Adam. So I search
for a missing rib. Yet a sweep of my fingers
reveals that all is intact. Even the memory
of my mother telling me the same about
Creation. About being alone.

> Basotho wedding
> wondering how
> they ululate

Women surround me now. They are worn
but strong. The workers. Keeping home

and hearth. Rearing children. Creation in every act. Yet this is no Eden. No Tigris or Euphrates. Pishon or Gihon. Here flow the Senqu and Makhaleng. Rivers in and through ragged mountains. Where an old woman takes me by the arm. Pulls me into some primordial dance.

    with each step
    knowing god
    is a she

Waxing, Waning

Yes, I say. I used to play football. American football. But the orphans in this distant place do not understand. Kick me the soccer ball anyway. I feign competence. Botch the return pass. They collect the ball. Giggle a bit. Scatter to their rooms before dinner. I watch after them. Wonder if I could still manage a gridiron tackle.

> winter solstice
> through the cracks in my life
> a sudden wind

I turn. Head to my own quarters. Curtains not yet drawn, I spy the rising moon from within. Hoping for a hot shower. Pondering still that tackle. Thinking my odds for either fifty-fifty.

> lunar rille
> here too no water
> remains

Metta[1]

When I cross the invisible boundary that divides the males and females in our dining hall to sit with the head caregiver at the end of yet another a long day, we become mother and father of this place. We bond in our affection for these children. Talk of them as if they were our own. Worry their illnesses and transgressions. Take pride in their accomplishments. She a Basotho widow and I a failed monk. So odd the ways of love.

> the heave
> and ho
> of a broken heart

---

1. *Metta* is the Pali term meaning "loving-kindness" and is practiced as a Buddhist meditation on compassion.

Ricochet

The marble slips from his jacket pocket. Bounce, bounce, bounces toward me. Rolls to a stop against my booted foot. He halts his playful chase. Looks up. Afraid. *No games in the dining hall.* A rule he has learned well. But this, I know, is an innocent mishap. I grin. Lift up to his tiny hand the blue orb flecked with gold. He offers in return a tentative tooth. Before a full-mouthed smile.

> winter wind
> the clack
> of an orphan's crutch

Water Witching

Somewhere a typhoon. A tropical storm. A hurricane. But here the waterbirds circle a desiccated pond. The villagers scout a dying spring. Together we dig ever deeper in search of our essential element. In search of some shared future.

> parched sunset
> slow swivel
> of the dowsing rods

Antipodal

Between winter and spring, August. All wind and sudden swings in Celsius. The moon sets as I wake. Walk dark paths toward the temple, where incense burns already. My gaze cast toward some distant horizon. The unknown unknown.

How many mornings since I arrived? Till I depart? What good have I done?

> first light
> Orion plunges
> into a sigh

Johannesburg: A Reprise

Even for an unplanned check-up, it is good to leave the orphanage. All work and no play. Eyes weary from the monitor. From the too long hours. The too many dilemmas. I rest them now on the passing scenes. The agrarian and the poverty of the Free State. And the motion in the back seat.

> out the car window
> grasping at clouds
> the orphan boy

We cross into Gauteng. Traffic thickens. The day wanes. But the boy seems to strengthen.

> Soweto highway
> in the roadside heaps
> a hint of gold

Then into it. The modern shopping malls. Footpaths leading away from them. Toward shanties. Somewhere in between terraced pubs transfigured into mega churches. He watches the crowds. Smiles.

> Johannesburg
> black smoke rising
> into ibis wings

Spring has arrived here. Just a slight chill at twilight. Around the burning rubbish heaps, a squatters' camp. Thin plastic tarps rustle around scavenged timber. A dark bottle passes hand to hand. He frowns. Turns away from "home."

> weaver's nest
> even in the dark
> a hint of life

In the Wind

It passes through the cracks around my worn door. The dust of ages covers all. My cups and books and clothes. This journal and pen. Nothing is left untouched. Save time itself.

> gusting moon
> the sudden sigh
> of peach blossoms

The shepherds knew of the coming change. Whispered it to the dawn. The seasons mark their movements. Shade their skin. Notch their bones. And cradle their flocks.

> *Basutoland*[1]
> behind the herder's shawl
> a lamb's eyes

---

1. *Basutoland* is the former colonial name for Lesotho.

Time on Earth

Now in the full throes of a season out of true. Still the greening of everything. The slow fatting of the sheep.

> too late
> rains drone anthropocene
> in an African timbre

I watch them from my stoop. The flocks. The young boys and old men tending them. Thin arms emerging from worn winter shawls. Making a haul of this late day light before the cold night. They move together from the watering hole to the rain-wetted donga. Where tender sprouts emerge only to be sheared by hungry teeth.

> one last bleat
> dark on the horizon
> shepherds wave

Earth and sky draw closer. This windblown plain reveals how little man has learned. How swiftly tinkling bells are muted.

human nature
a single contrail cuts
the great twilight sky

I Take the Threatening Stick

. . . from the fist of the teacher. Ask the child to hold onto each end. Grip between her tiny hands and lift her up. Past my chest and neck. By the time her eyes reach mine tears have dried. A frown become a smile. Then higher. Over my head. All squeals and laughter. The others, too. Queuing up for the next take-off.

> learning how
> to hold a pencil
> blossom moon

Confucius & the Sangoma

The orphans are flummoxed by their foreign benefactors. So many unfamiliar rules here. *No hands in pockets. Hold your bowl with a dragon's maw grip. Bow to every teacher. To begin class. To end it.* These dictates too often tangled in the word rather than the spirit. But slowly the edicts of Confucius fade on the photocopied sheet pasted to the classroom wall. The drums beyond the compound fence sound again. The children listen. Hear the sangoma commune with the spirits of their ancestors. Understand fragments of the shaman's prophecy. And begin to remember where they are. Who they are.

cooing
African pigeons
under the day moon

African Time

The wild creatures I had come to Africa to see are exhilarating in their multitudes and colors, and I imagined for a time that this glimpse of the earth's morning might account for the anticipation that I felt, the sense of origins, of innocence and mystery, like a marvelous childhood faculty restored.

— Peter Matthiessen
The Tree Where Man Was Born

And yet after years on the continent I remain inside some compound of foreignness. At night the ancestors call to me. Not the dead. But the living voices of the internal. Of past lives and those we've met along the path. Again and again.

> slow sifting
> through my hands
> moonbeams

The universe sings to us, if only we will listen. Remove the distracting noise. Step outside the external. Onto the ground of it all. One slow step then another. A steady dance with our karma. Step becomes song. Becomes this.

> slow surge
> of the swallowtail
> African spring

Karma

We gather in the day's laundry. Our scattered selves also back into community. *Motho ke motho ka batho!*[1] Together finding a way. Our way. So many collective barriers. Here a washed out bridge. There a rockslide wall. Yet we flow. Under and over. And toward.

> lightning strike
> beyond the horizon
> a child's dream

1. *Motho ke motho ka batho* is a Basotho proverb meaning, *A person is a person through other people.*

The Sky Is Falling

We race stride for stride. But my horses overcome theirs. A simple matter of numbers rather than skill or power. More than two hundred to three. A Land Cruiser versus a trio of Basotho ponies. Their riders in woven hats and thick shawls. Bareback. Me in the soft leather seat, old jeans and a Phillies cap turned backwards. I pass them by all too soon.

> touching the sun
> last ride
> of the dying chief

The final bit of sky settles red in the donga's shimmer. The shepherds and their flocks long departed. A single mule on the horizon. Unmoving. And so the earth and sky move around him. I envy his stillness. Wonder at what I have lost. At what I might never find.

bowed acacia
just one
African wagtail

Making a Life

I slowly come to imagine myself here forever. Half monk. Half father. Learning to be a leader. Conjuring some vision of harmony—local staff, overseas volunteers and the children bound together in purpose. I allow myself to settle ever deeper. To sprout roots. Friends and familiar faces. Connections at other NGOs. In government offices. On the street.

> the hawker
> adds an extra mango
> summer breeze

Then the sudden news of discord at the organization's headquarters. A mass resignation from our board of directors, including my mentor. She writes of a negation of the reforms we had begun. Shares concerns about the founder's vision. I am left wondering, again, about right livelihood.

first plane out
my bags half full
half empty

After Words

Causes and Conditions

I came here to Africa, Buddha. I offered three bows. Three sticks of incense. Three years. I have repented. Offered again and again three prostrations. And repent still.

on a faraway ridge
still no closer
to the moon

Tea with the Nun

"What will you do now?" she asks.
"I will teach."
"Where?"
"Yes. Where?"
"I have friends in Malaysia."
"Malaysia then."

      silence
      how the river
      bends it

haiku talk —
counting the bugs
in the overhead lamps

long titles
from long poems
from the long lecture

Kuti
Johor, Malaysia

3:50am. My wristwatch alarm.

Yesterday at Santi Forest Monastery this would have been followed by the bell sounding out into the darkness. Well before the distant call of the muezzin. Mosquitos would have been buzzing at the screens of my meager kuti. Somewhere in the surrounding tangle of oil palms a macaque would bay. No birdsong yet. But it would come. The great bell would continue its toll. Silence all else. Vibrations would wax and wane. Wax again. Out into this movement the half-moon emerging from thick clouds. My shuffling steps. The world all sound and vibration. I would remove my sandals before the first of the stairs. Climb to the hall. Enter with a bow. Find the way to my mat. Offer three prostrations. Pull into half-lotus. And still the bell. The vibrations. Toward awareness and clarity. Soon the last toll. The final pulse dissolving into the forest, the hall, the monks and into me. Then I in turn a slow dissipation into the monks, the hall, the forest. Only breath remaining.

Today, here in my Monday-morning flat, I move from bed to kitchen to that same mat. A bow and three prostrations. Incense. A brief Dharma reading. Then the same half-lotus. Stillness in the awareness of movement. The breath. The breath. The breath.

There Phra Ajaan Keng would break the silence with the first line of the Pali sutta. The other monks and lay practitioners would join in. Here I invoke the guardian deity Tara in Sanskrit. Finish with the *Heart Sutra* in Korean. There another bell would signal the day's first meal. Here a second alarm moves me from mat to kitchen to the preparation of oats and coffee. To the shower. To school. To the sleepy smiles of my students.

To a life, perhaps and finally, with some balance. With two truths held simultaneously.

> where willow
> meets bamboo
> wind music

Publication Credits

"Non-Stop" *Ephemerae* 1C

"Johannesburg" *Contemporary Haibun Online* 6.13

"Muti" *Contemporary Haibun Online* 11.4

"Township" *Contemporary Haibun Online* 9.3

"Weekends at a Zen Orphanage" (first published as "Malawi Orphanage") *Modern Haiku* 49.1

"Africa Cup" *The Mamba* 5

"Indulgence" *Ephemerae* 1A

"Witching Hour" *Haibun Today* 12.4

"Macadamia" previously unpublished, with the haiku and sections of prose in "The Seed" first published as "Under the Silk Scarf" in *Contemporary Haibun Online* 14.3

"The Rains of Malawi" *The Mamba* 10

"Bodhisattva Path" (first published as "Bodhisattva") *Contemporary Haibun Online* 16.3

"A Different Word for It" *Contemporary Haibun Online* 14.2

"No Place for Evil" *The Mamba* 6

"Settling In" *The Mamba* 6

"American Independence Day in Lesotho" *Frogpond* 41.3

"The Binding String" *Cattails* April 2019

"Triple Refuge" *Cattails* October 2018

"Bone of My Bones" *Ephemerae* 1C

"Ricochet" *Red River Book of Haibun* 1

"Water Witching" *Contemporary Haibun Online* 14.4

"Johannesburg: A Reprise" *Contemporary Haibun Online* 15.1

"Time on Earth" *Frogpond* 42.3

"I Take the Threatening Stick" *Modern Haiku* 50.1

"Confucius & the Sangoma" *Haibun Today* 13.4

"African Time" *Haibun Today* 13.3

"Karma" (first published as "African Karma") *The Mamba* 7

"The Sky is Falling" *Haibun Today* 13.1

All others previously unpublished.

Acknowledgments

The list of those who've helped along this project in some meaningful way is extensive. Yet in addition to the children and care mothers of the Amitofo Care Centers, some merit a special mention. This collection began as a renunciation guided and supported by Venerable Chungho Sunim of Musimsa Temple in New York City. Became an African sojourn enriched through the counsel of Miaohong Shifu. Was inspired by the constant querying of my ACC Lesotho assistant Selloane Masiloane. Took its first form as a book during a spell at the Buddhist Retreat Center in Ixopo, South Africa. Grew in scope and scale thanks to early readings by Antony and Margie Osler at Poplar Grove Zen Center in the Great Karoo of South Africa. Was refined through later scrutiny and assessment by poet Dawn Garisch of Cape Town. And has been gifted the evocative cover by Beata Somogyi of Zalaapati, Hungary.

My Pennsylvania family offered always a perfect refuge for reflection and writing. The editors at the journals in which many of these pieces were first published provided insight and encouragement. And, of course, Jim Kacian at Red Moon Press brought this book to life.

A deep bow of gratitude to them and to all I've met along the way.

Before his renunciation, **Matthew Caretti** had been teaching English literature and composition at the university and high school levels for nearly twenty years. Time in Africa included assignments as a Peace Corps Volunteer and at the Amitofo Care Centers. His pilgrimage now continues by means of work as an itinerant teacher.